WHISKEY MOTH

WHISKEY MOTH

by A.M. Wegelin

Paperclip Publishing, LLC
Chandler, AZ

Whiskey Moth

Copyright © 2022 by A.M. Wegelin

Published by: Paperclip Publishing LLC

Editor: Noelle S. LeBlanc
Cover Design: Keenan S. Peebles
Interior Typography: Hannah Thigpen

Library of Congress Control Number: 2022938865

ISBN: 979-8-88589-207-0 (paperback)

ISBN: 979-8-88589-206-3 (hardcover)

ISBN: 979-8-88589-208-7 (eBook)

Printed in Rephen Printing, Co. LTD in Guangzhou and the United States of America

First Printing: 2022

Paperclip Publishing LLC
3800 W Ray Road Suite 5
Chandler, AZ 85226

www.paperclippublishing.com

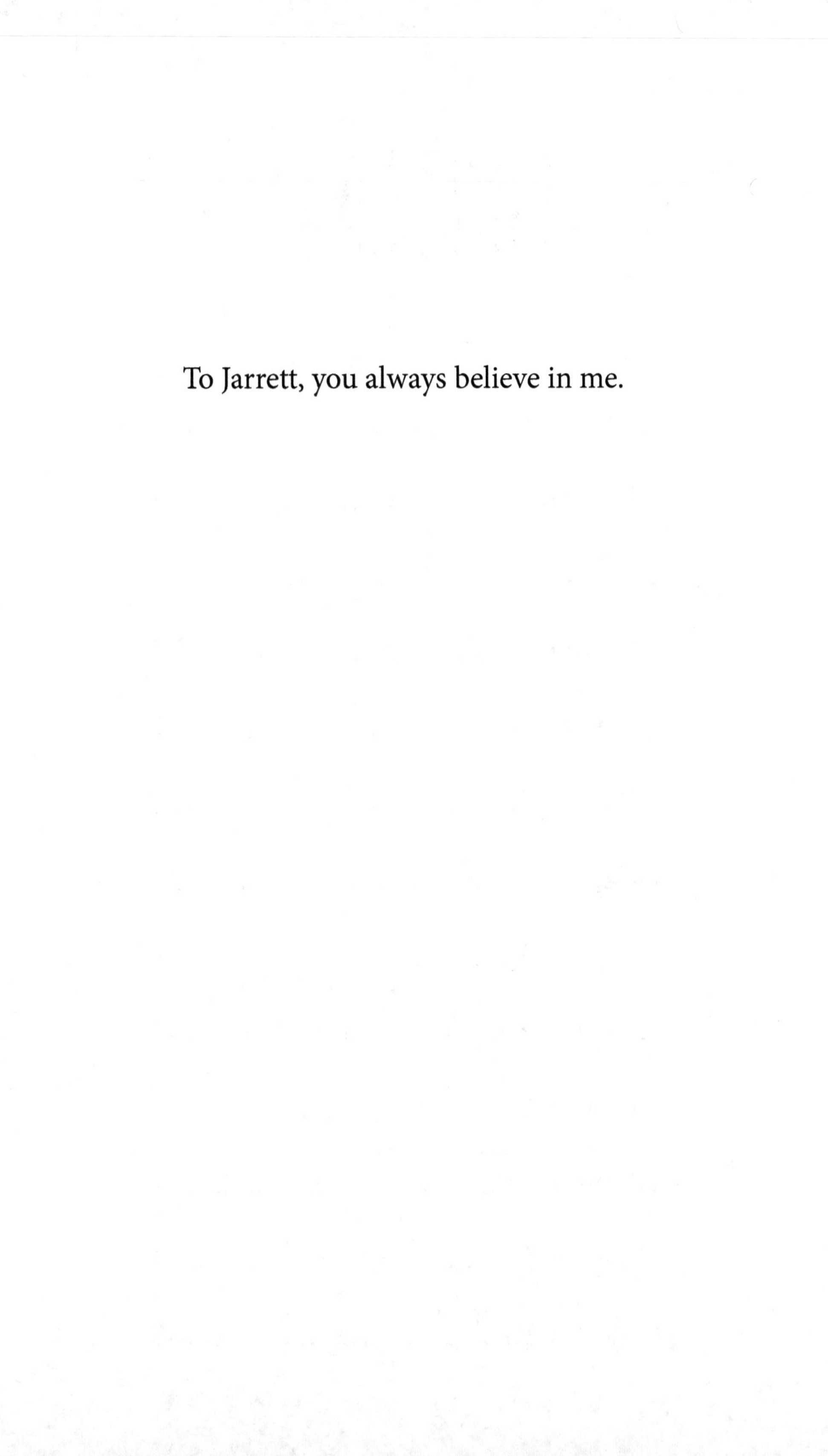

To Jarrett, you always believe in me.

CONTENTS

This place smells like rot. You see all the pretty pictures they put up on the website, where the sun is hitting everything just right and you believe you've found home. Instead, you've found a place that smells like rot. In the two minutes I've been here, I've already seen a small family of cockroaches that have long since expired. Maybe it was the rot stink that killed them. OR maybe this place is so toxic that they just died on impact, making the same poor choice I made when moving here. I can see it now, the mom cockroach clasping the tiny bug hands of her children while the daddy cockroach sniffs out the nearest source of nasty for their next infestation. He comes upon this terrible hellhole and announces to his family that they have found a home. Before he can even finish his sentence, his tiny bug lungs fill up with asbestos and they all die a horrible, horrible death. In memoriam of this family's tragedy, I try to sweep them under the door with my foot while humming "Amazing Grace".

If I could rate this place on a scale of one to ten, I would rate it gross.

I would do anything to turn back time right now but, to my complete dismay, I am stuck with this studio apartment for at least a year. Damn you, lease. Damn you, mother who knew this would happen, and yet I never listened to because I have never listened to anything that's come out of her mouth. Why would anyone listen to his or her mom when at the prime age for stupid decisions anyway? The promise of one day being able to move to California was the only thing that kept me from jumping off a bridge through my crap childhood. I mean, seriously, who in their right mind would settle their family in the Midwest? Do they want us to grow up obese and content with utter mediocrity? No, they just love cheap housing and low expectations. Selfish motherfuckers.

I come from a lovely little town called Oak Forest, Illinois. By lovely I mean overrun with chunky babies and pizza parlors. Oh, and don't forget the terrible weather, ignorance, racism, and barrels of sad women going to trade school to be nurses because they had a baby at nineteen with a guy that is now MIA. I know what you are thinking, *Oh, Michelle, tell us how you REALLY feel.* Ha. Great joke. You sound like my dad, and that is something you should be ashamed of because he was an old, middle-class, white guy from the Midwest. That is statistically the worst thing you could possibly be.

By this point, I'm sure you can tell that I'm very good at complaining and being negative. I make a sport out of it; I'd be a gold medal winner if they had it as an event in the Olympics. It's probably why I had no friends in Oak Forest. In fact, I think everywhere would find me pretty intolerable. I am Michelle, queen of being unwanted. Let the pity party begin.

Standing in front of my pile of boxes, I dread every second ahead of me. I must open each and every one and put the contents somewhere in this awful, horrible, disgusting place. Sounds like the worst. Instead, I stare out the window of my downtrodden home and look into the abyss that is the ghetto of Long Beach. I have a lovely view of a street where homeless people seem to only multiply every time I blink. Blink. 2. Blink. 4. Blink. 37. Are these homeless people or is this just how everyone looks here?

I open my first box and only see my failure displayed before me. A few pieces of clothing, some plates, a bunch of junk that I mistakenly thought was important, and a tin full of my mother's cookies because she insisted that, it being so close to Christmas, I needed to take them. 'Who could possibly celebrate Christmas without cookies?' I could almost hear in her syrupy, nagging tone that only the vagina that bore you can pull off. I sigh heavily to no one and throw the clothing on the floor. I'll deal with it later. By 'deal with', I mean complain about it later and let it just become one with the floor. One of the plates calls to me and I stare at it for an inordinate amount of time. It still has food crusted on it because my ex-boyfriend washed the dishes before I left and he sucks at everything. He probably felt like he didn't have to try anymore since I was leaving him for beach air and an abundance of surfer abs. Because that's all Illinoisians think California is like. I had no idea I was in for rotting air and homeless abs. He never really cared about much anyway. He spent a good portion of his time shutting me out and playing Call Of Duty like it was his only escape from what a boring, lame human being he was.

For a minute, I feel like crying. I really don't like to cry and I try to do it as little as possible. A tear escapes my dumb eye-hole, and I want to crawl up in a blanket ball like I did when I was a kid. Unfortunately, I have no blankets unpacked so this is impossible, which just makes me panic more. I pull the tin of cookies out and open it. Inside are Snickerdoodles. Of course they're Snickerdoodles. My goddamn thoughtful mother packed my goddamn favorite cookie. I shove a handful in my mouth and sob once before shutting down. I can't cry. Crying means I'm weak, and if I'm weak then I'll never respect myself. I don't even know why I am crying. Well, I mean, it could be that I moved thousands of miles away from the only people who love me and I have no idea what I'm doing…but I will discount that as nothing because denial is way more comforting than the truth.

The last time I really cried was at my father's funeral. A classy event with lots of sniveling mourners, just the way he would have liked it. Much to my sweet mother's and my dismay, his gaggle of office sluts showed up too. I cried when my mother wouldn't come out of the coat closet. She is the biggest bear of a woman I know, and seeing her breakdown was too much for my usually cold heart. She carried my brother and me through some of the toughest times in our lives. She loved me even after I came home drunk and covered in mud when I was sixteen because I decided that dating a college boy was a good idea. He decided the good idea was to pour beer after beer down my throat until I blacked out, laughing at the fact I couldn't handle my booze. I still don't remember a good chunk of what happened that night but maybe that's for the best. She loved me through all the violent outbursts, the pill-popping, the reckless behavior, and the hysteric tantrums. She is the only thing keeping me from imploding, and I left her.

I open the next box and pull out a half-empty bottle of vodka. Bottom shelf, just the way I like it. You know the kind, the one in the clear plastic bottle with some Russian name. I open it and gag at the smell before trying to take a sip. I'm terrible at drinking liquor straight, and immediately it comes rushing back up my throat. I spit it up on my floor and groan. I have no paper towels so I just use a shirt I threw on the ground and try to mop it up. I'm disgusting, a disgusting pig. I eat another handful of cookies and try to take another swig. It stays down this time, and I feel victorious for the first time today. I continue my cookie-drinking process until the whole bottle is gone and I am sufficiently drunk. With a light head and a lighter heart, I open another box and then another.

"I am Cleopatra. I am Aphrodite. I can do anything."

I flex in the bathroom mirror. I feel powerful and motivated. Something is missing though. I dig through my purse until I find that wonderful orange bottle. My God. Xanax. It's amazing what a doctor will prescribe when you throw yourself on the floor of their office and bang your fists on the ground like a child that was denied candy at the supermarket. I pop two pills and unpack my record player. The record player I bought when I first started dating my ex so he would think I was some kind of retro sex goddess. I put on my Ziggy Stardust record and start tearing empty boxes in half as if I was Godzilla destroying a city of cardboard.

"PUSHING THROUGH THE MARKET SQUARE..."

I am now scream-singing "Five Years" like the seasoned Bowie fan I am. After a couple more songs of air piano, headbanging, and passionately faking my way through the lyrics my alcohol-addled brain refuses to remember, I start to get restless. I feel so powerful and in control. I want more. I want to drink until I pass out. I dig through my pile of unpacked clothing until I find the one dress I don't feel like a monster-cow in and pull it over my head. This is it, the big night. I'm going to find true love; I'm going to blow the world apart. Everyone will want to be my friend and laugh at my clever anecdotes. I slip my feet into my dirty, worn flats and open my apartment door. The night air feels cold and, instead of the musty smell of my apartment, the ocean breeze hits me. I step into it and over my sad cockroach family, enveloped in the freeing feeling of being alive. I am young and stupid. For a second I love it.

The Deaf Horse is renowned for its huge selection of whiskey. Whiskey upon whiskey. About a hundred choices so you can come in every day for a year and never drink the same kind. They even have moonshine, which is something I have never understood the appeal of as it just reminds me of paint thinner. I am also kind of obsessed the second I walk in the door with their Mortal Kombat machine because it's the only game I could ever beat my brother at. My only secret was to button mash faster than he could do combos, but hey, I was a winner for a brief moment. On my first night, I stumble in, high off of my own intoxicating, alcohol-induced confidence and Xanax. I take a look at the rustic feel of the place and eye their smiling patronage. The place is relatively packed and there is a single empty seat at the bar just beckoning to be sat in. I lurch forward into the seat and grab one of their menus. A menu loaded with the nectar of the gods. I try to focus my eyes on the small type and must have looked like a psycho, holding the menu at arm's length and squinting with a clear look of 'Help, I have no idea what's going on.'

"Hey, darling, what will you have?"

I normally hate when people call me 'darling' or 'sweetheart', but the look on the bartender's face was too warm for me to come back with a snotty comment.

"Wass good?" I slurred. "Forget it, I'm sure you're sick of hearing that question. Give me a whiskey sour."

"I'll be right back." She smiled thickly at me.

While I awaited the drink that would surely fulfill my need for further inebriation, I glanced around again at the bar to see if anyone would fulfill my need for dicking. Much to my dismay, it was mostly dudes that decided their mustaches needed to be taken care of more than their body odor. They all look like they smell of my apartment. I start laughing to myself at the thought since I am my biggest fan when it comes to my inside-brain jokes. The bartender was back by the time I wiped my eyes because I laughed so hard at myself.

"You alright, sweet pea?"

"Yeah, yeah, I'm just so funny. I really kill myself sometimes."

She looked at me with one eyebrow raised and then giggled. "Where you from?"

"The Midwest."

"You sound like it."

She walked away, shaking her head a bit but still wearing that awfully kind smile that just sucked me in. Maybe, for once, I could charm someone into being my friend, even if it's one of those distant friends that you talk to once a month and say 'we should hang out!' even though you never will. I'm THAT kind of desperate.

"YOU WANNA BE MY FRIEND?!" I blurt from my stool. Shit, shit, shit. I want to make friends, and instead she's gonna think I'm a loud drunk-ass. I mean, I DO need friends so I don't die from loneliness, but I think this was the dumbest way to try and get one.

She turns around and yells back, "WHAT?"

I now shrink back into my skin and look away, but she is onto me. She slinks back over and leans against the bar.

"What did you say? I couldn't hear you over the music."

"OHHH, nothing. It's cool. I'm sorry."

"Why are you apologizing?"

"I yelled. I yelled like a big dumb lug. I'm a fucking monster. I'M A MONSTER."

At this point, most of the bar is looking at me. I am in drunken-rage mode. I AM a monster. I wanna stomp on everyone and crush their brains out of their awful skulls. I wanna suffocate them with their mustaches.

I crack a smile through what must be a terrible expression of fury and insanity and force out a laugh because I'm being ridiculous. The bartender looks mildly horrified but in the way that she is at least entertained.

"What's your name?" I yell over the noise.

"Cleo. What's yours?"

"Michelle. I don't have any friends here. I just moved here today."

"Sweetheart, I'm not qualified to have this discussion. I dropped out of community college for god sakes, and I know us bartenders are supposed to lend an ear but—"

"No, no, no…. I uh. I GOTTA GO."

I leave a crumpled twenty on the bar, enough to pay for my drink and my outburst, and then I peel myself off the stool. I turn my head before she can make eye contact again and dart for the door. I'm acting like I'm asking a boy out or something. This is fucking stupid. I'll just be friendless-psycho-face forever. I'll roam the country, creeping out nice bartenders until the end of time. What a life. I light a cigarette as I walk down the street back to the ol' stinkhole. Man, this day couldn't get any more awful. I mean, unless my biggest fear comes true where some icky guy kidnaps me and puts me in his basement where he repeatedly rapes me for years. Hey, it happens.

I wake up to the sun hitting me through my cheap, vertical, plastic blinds. It's blinding and painful, the way that waking up covered in shards of glass would be. Wait. Am I covered in shards of glass? I rub my body and try to lift my head to see. Wrong decision because the shooting pain starts. Oh jeez. I really am feeling the cookie-drunk that I participated in last night. Then I remember what happened at the bar. Fuck. I was just full of it last night. That poor bartender had no idea what hit her. In all actuality, she probably doesn't even remember me, which is the most painful part. I'd rather be remembered as a weird freak of nature than not remembered at all. Like how you wish your ex kept your naked pictures instead of deleting them like you never existed. And don't you dare judge me about that because we all think those thoughts. I put my head back down on my pillow and moan.

"I am NOT Cleopatra. I am NOT Aphrodite. I am just sad, human waste."

I seriously consider falling back asleep. Then it dawns on me. Go back to the bar! Maybe Cleo is working and I can make amends! Wait a minute, this is insane. She's going to have me thrown out and condemned for being a stalker. My sad future begins, a giant tree trunk of a bouncer grabbing me by the scruff of my neck and tossing me out into the street to be an outcast for eternity. I am being overdramatic and I roll around on the bed snarling,

"What do I do? What do I do? Lord have mercy, what do I do?"

I sit up suddenly and suffer the immense consequences. The pain courses through my head and wracks my body. I figure I am already this far so I try and stand up, which results in my legs quivering like a newborn deer. Staggering around, I reach my pile of clothing and I haggardly pull out the first thing that resembles something someone might wear that would be acceptable in society. It's a flowery dress because all my pants don't fit my huge ass anymore. I pull it on clumsily and pray that I don't topple over. I stare into the mirror and take in the full horror that is my face. My eyes stare back at me with a bitter, pleading expression, and it looks like I haven't slept in weeks. This could also just be the effect of my eyeliner smudged around both of my granite countertop–colored eyes. At least that's what my ex always said my eyes looked like—granite fucking countertops. How incredibly fucking romantic. Just like everything he did. I can't tell you how many anniversaries I got something that was more for him than me. Like a Playstation 4. OHHHH wow, thanks for nothing. 'Oh, but Michelle, I thought you looooved video games.' No. No, I don't. It's just a present of watching you play hours of them while I do housework. How fucking thoughtful.

I lick my thumb and rub it on one of my eyelids. This just seems to exacerbate the problem, and I shrug at myself. Sorry, me, you look like you crawled out of a dumpster after a long night of prostituting for meth money. I go into the bathroom and splash water on my face, rubbing my eyes and when I look up at myself, the problem has once again been made worse. My eyeliner is now running down my decaying face as though I cried forever, emphasizing all my premature aging caused by the pack of cancer I inhale on a daily basis. I use a towel that I dabbed in soap and rub even harder on my poor, puffy eyes. It finally starts to come off. I'm only twenty-three and my face is already starting to fall apart. With my makeup gone, I am breathing in the full effect of my complexion. Covered in red splotches, acne, and dry skin, I truly wish I could peel off my face and reveal something more appealing.

"I hate you," I whisper to myself. I think I might have a minor self-esteem problem. Just another thing that I can ignore in my life instead of confronting it like a grown woman.

I apply a fresh coat of lies to my skin and take the curling iron to my unruly frizz that some might call 'hair'. Some people say, 'Hey, you should be lucky you have such beautiful curly hair,' but you have no idea how much the nickname 'poodle head' ruins it for a young girl. My hair is a weird mixture of the colors auburn and blonde with the roots half grown in. Everyone thinks, 'Oooh! Ombre!' I think, 'Ooooh! I stopped caring a long time ago.'

I am finally put together, and I breathe in the sense of relief that floats around me like a thick cloud of vanity. I am ready to go mop up my shame.

Cleo is here. She is standing out front, smoking a cigarette. A wave of crippling anxiety washes over me as I approach her. My heart is beating out of my chest and I cough heavily into my sleeve. This gains her attention, and I smile bashfully, which probably looks more like the crazed teeth display a serial killer uses to calm his victims so they get into his van. "What am I, some kind of shameless creep?" I whisper to myself, unable to break my strange expression. Walking over to her, I try putting on the guise of 'chill' by puffing on my own cigarette nonchalantly and I attempt to break the ice as casually as I can muster.

"Hey, sorry for my behavior last night.... I was being a mess."

"It's alright, sweetheart. I work in a bar, you think I don't see girls like you every night?"

"Ha. I was drunk and—"

"Of course you were. What else do people do in bars?"

"Uhm…go on awful dates they meet online, hang out with friends, sit alone, and think about all they've done wrong in their lives?"

She laughs sincerely and winks at me. "But they always get drunk."

"You're right, I'm just ashamed of existing."

"You wanna come inside? First round is on me." She flicks her cigarette butt into the street and starts climbing down the stairs that lead into the whiskey haven. I follow suit and clasp my hands together in excitement and intense gratefulness at this wonderful bartender's gentle demeanor. We enter the dimly lit cellar of the establishment, and she gets behind the counter.

"I've got just what you want, darling."

She starts mixing a concoction of ginger beer, whiskey, and lemon. She adds a sprig of thyme just for taste and hands the chilled glass to me.

"Try this, tell me what you think."

I take a long swig and wipe my mouth. It's delicious and full of flavors that somehow swirl together to make the perfect beverage. This is dangerous, and I start chugging this godly mixture down my cigarette-wrecked throat.

"Oh dear god, make me another."

She laughs wholeheartedly and starts making another. "This one is on you now."

"That's fine, I've got that sweet life insurance money."

"Oh yeah? Better be careful. Don't want it to run out."

"Oh, it's going to. I spent most of it just getting here." She hands me another glass, and I down it just as fast as the first. I am feeling loosey-goosey from the drinks because she mixed them so strong and I start giggling to myself again. My craziness just gets amplified ten-fold when I get drunk. "So, on a serious note, do you have any job openings?"

"Sorry, hunny, but we are fully staffed at the moment. Also, you kinda need a license to be a bartender."

"Jeez Louise. How's a girl supposed to eat?"

"Have you tried applying for jobs around the city yet?"

"I hate food service, I hate retail, and pretty much everyone plus everything."

"Why would you want to be a bartender then?"

"Watching people make terrible decisions—and tips."

"Well, just between you and me, there's some other ways to make money.... Not honorable ways but ways."

"Oh please don't try and turn me into a sex slave. I already have nightmares about it. Is that bouncer guy the pimp?! Oh jeez."

"Oh no no. Way less honorable than that."

She had my attention. "Please, do tell what this is."

She leaned over the bar and looked both ways before leaning even closer to whisper, "Well, there's this guy that comes into the bar every night and buys underwear off girls."

"…What the living fuck does that even mean?"

"This guy comes into this very bar and buys dirty underwear off of girls. They go into the bathroom and take them off, and then he buys them for fifty dollars." She starts making me another drink. "And that's all you gotta do, just be a girl that wears panties and is willing to degrade herself."

"Ugh, don't use the word 'panties', it's such a disgusting word."

"You have no room to be making those requests right now. You are considering selling your *unmentionables*. Better?" She hands me the new drink and I down it in almost one gulp.

"Better. I have to think about it. That's a weird fucking thing to do."

"I get it. Just think about it." She winks at me and goes to help another patron that is growing increasingly impatient with Cleo giving me all the attention. I am floored, baffled, bewildered, and other sorts of emotions. Fifty dollars for a measly pair of underwear? I would never have to get a real job. I could just live in squalor at my dingy stinkhole. Ahhh, the sweet life. Cleo comes back over to me and sets another full glass of heaven juice in front of me, which I swallow in a couple of huge gulps. "So, Michelle, what are you doing later? Like…around eight?" Cleo eyes me wearily.

"Rolling around in my own filth, why?"

"You should come over. I have a huge collection of vinyl, a cute cat, and more booze."

"Done. Where do you live?"

She writes her address on a bar napkin, and I pocket the thing. I smile the biggest smile anyone has had the pleasure of seeing, leave some twenties, and tip an imaginary hat to her like a big fucking neck-beard douchebag as I slither out of the bar.

It's eight o'clock, and I'm standing in front of Cleo's apartment. I'm too on time, which is giving me unreasonable anxiety. I don't want to seem too thrilled about this potential friendship, so I hang back to smoke a cigarette. As I light it up, Cleo comes out onto her balcony. I suppose great minds think alike. She sees me before she takes her first drag and waves ecstatically at me. I'm caught in the act. Dammit.

"Throw your cigarette up and come inside!"

"Throw it?! All the way up there??"

"Yes! Come on!"

I toss my lit cigarette, and it lands without setting her on fire. I go up to the gate tentatively. Normally you have to use a code to get in, but it's clearly broken, so I just push the knob and it opens. What great security this place has. I take the stairs two at a time until I get to the second floor. Unit 5. The 5 on the door is hanging at a weird angle and there are a few dents as if the cops had kicked it in a few times too many. The paint is crudely applied, peeling, and uninviting. This harbinger of disgustingness comes swinging open, and a beaming Cleo stands on the other side. "Well, well. You showed up."

"Of course I showed up."

"Come in!"

I enter a cozy-looking living room full of furniture that doesn't match at all, which is actually quite charming and goes well with the light wooden floors while also triggering my insane OCD. The walls are a forest green, and several strings of lights hang from the ceiling. Sitting by the television, there is a cage with a rather large, colorful chameleon sitting inside. On the walls are several paintings; one of them is a giant version of a naked lady that has the head of a deer. She sees me staring at it with a completely awed expression.

"That's a self-portrait."

"It's lovely," I mutter, gawking at the incredible detail and beautiful brush-strokes. The deer woman is looking into my soul; I have to tear my eyes away.

Against the walls are giant vintage-looking chairs that are all different colors and patterns. The promised 'cute cat' sits in one of them, a fat bag of fur that has brilliant green eyes. It flips its tail back and forth at the sight of me and jumps down, hiding behind the giant arcade game in the corner. Buster Brothers. I had never heard of the game before and walk over to it, eyeing the massive thing cautiously.

"Uh...Why?" I point at it and smile coyly, expecting to get some conversation out of it, to break the uncomfortable silence.

"I hold the world record." She lifts her shirt up to reveal a tattoo of the game's character on her ribs. "2,430,023 points." She smiles sheepishly back.

"Wow. That's insane. Why, though? Like, why do you have the world record?"

"I wanted to be the best at something."

"Why Buster Brothers? Why not Space Invaders or something?"

"Easier to get the high score. Fewer people to compete against."

Seemingly done with this topic, she turns away from me and walks back out onto the balcony. I follow suit, assuming I was invited too to finish my cigarette. Upon walking outside, I notice my cigarette has already burned halfway down and the ash is piling up. I stomp it out, put the butt in the ashtray next to Cleo, and light another. We sit down and bask in silence for a moment, puffing away at our poison. Some people are suicidal. And some are more cleverly so. I just am choosing not to get old.

Cleo laughs. I smile in response and tilt my head as if to ask why. She shakes her head. "I just don't normally invite customers to my apartment. This is just weird for me. I feel awkward."

"If you feel too awkward I can go...."

"No, I like you. You're a cutie pie."

"I uhm, I like you too. I just don't really know how to do this. The talking and being sociable."

"Let's drink first."

Cleo slinks inside and I am not sure whether to follow her. Instead, I stay outside smoking. I am nervous now, petrified really. My stomach feels hollow, and I want to throw up. Alcohol is probably not the best thing to add to the picture. Cleo reappears with a bottle of wine and two glasses. She pours me a glass. I notice it's Chardonnay. My dad used to be really into wine and taught me everything there is to know about it. I try to ignore my brain going through the steps of a proper tasting and just down the glass. It's cheap anyway, what good would smelling it do? Cleo is staring at me, and I feel even more nervous than before. I hold my glass out to her and try to make my face give the appearance of a grin. I'm sure I just look like I have to shit or something.

"You have beautiful eyes, you know that?" She leans in. I want to hyper-ventilate. I want to crawl into the gutter and never come out. Is she hitting on me?

"Thank you," I whisper. I had experimented in college by kissing a few girls at drunken parties but I never went past that curiosity. Is this why she invited me here? Not to be my friend but get in my pants? My self-confidence is crushed and simultaneously lifted. I am confused. I am freaking the fuck out. Calm down. Maybe she is just being nice. Then she leans even closer.

"I've never fucked a redhead before."

Okay, this is crazy. I am frozen in fear. I start stuttering like an idiot. "I-I d-don't uhm, this uhm, w-what?!"

"Are you okay?"

"I'm straight." I finally manage to blurt out.

"Oh dear god. What the fuck."

"I'm so sorry."

"Why on earth are you sorry?! I'm the one who assumed you were a les-bian! I am such a fucking asshole. I mean. Oh my god."

"I thought you wanted to be friends!"

"Oh sweet Jesus. I am *such* a fucking asshole."

"I just wanted to be friends...."

"We can just be friends! I'm so sorry."

Then there was silence. We both look intently at the other. Moments pass, it feels like hours.

"So, you wanna make out?"

I look at Cleo. She is a pretty girl. I need a friend. I sigh internally and put on a big, sensual smirk.

"Okay."

She gets up and straddles me on the rocking chair I'm sitting in. Her lips are warm and soft, she smells like wine. My dad used to smell like wine.

It's a Tuesday. At least I think it's a Tuesday. It's starting to get dark outside and this is usually the time I go to the Deaf Horse or I go to Cleo's, depending on her work schedule. It's been a week since I moved here and we already have a system. I wake up, I spend the day doing nothing, I hang out with Cleo, I make out drunkenly with Cleo, I go to sleep. This is my life. My mother would be so proud.

I have been on my laptop all day, doing nothing. I check my bank account for the thirtieth time today. It's still twenty-three dollars and five cents. The Deaf Horse has run me dry. With every cocktail costing ten dollars, I have run out of money quick. Rent isn't due for another three weeks, but with no real job in sight, I think back on what Cleo said about selling my underwear. I type into Google how to sell your underwear and am rewarded with a daunting twelve million and nine hundred thousand results. I close my laptop. How hard can it be? I'll just ask Cleo tonight. She isn't working, and the plan is to meet at her house and watch *Life Aquatic* for the third time, her favorite movie. Personally, if we are going the Wes Anderson route, I'd choose *Darjeeling Limited*, but she says Owen Wilson is far too annoying in that movie for it to be tolerable.

I stand up and my head starts to spin. I haven't eaten all day, except for a bag of chips that I bought from the gas station, and my body is punishing me for it. I never was very good at being healthy. My weight has significantly yo-yoed since I was about twelve years old. I bounce between 130 and 200 pounds easily in the course of a few months, and it's taken its toll on me. I used to punish myself by beating my body with a baseball bat when I was getting 'fat'. You may be thinking to yourself, *how in the hell did you do that??* but it is possible. Just ask your local scientist. Honestly, I've never been fat—even at 200 pounds my body carried the weight elegantly. It all went to my ass and breasts. But this didn't change how I would see myself in the mirror. I would only see a big fat chunkster. I'm on the heavier side right now, but hey, at least Cleo finds me attractive.

I pull on the same dress I've been wearing for the past few days, the floral one that I don't feel entirely too ooky in, and I grab my purse. The walk to Cleo's is short and scary. Full of homeless people asking for change and muttering under their breath about how I'm a bitch for not giving them any. I step outside and light a cigarette, as per usual, and walk down 5th Avenue. I am vibrant and full of energy, probably because I've been sitting on the couch all day. I breathe in the fumes of exhaust from passing cars. It truly is a lovely evening to be taking a stroll in Long Beach. I wave charmingly at passing strangers, to be received with only a mild nod or two. It's fine, I feel too giddy to be deterred by the gloom of their attitudes. I turn the corner at Pacific and I'm suddenly there, standing in front of the three-level apartment building and waving at a brilliant, shining Cleo. I am full of it tonight. She smiles and waves back, seemingly excited to see me. In her arms is the 'cute cat' whose name I finally learned, Pavlovia. She hisses and jumps down from her arms, climbing the balcony railing and sitting on the edge, glaring at me. Such a grumpy animal with a similarly grumpy name. I run up the stairs and into Cleo's waiting arms. I am home. Well, somewhat home. I am somewhere. Somewhere that I don't feel out of place or unwanted. I feel okay.

I bounce up and down. "Are you ready to watch the movie?!"

"Well, I thought we could make out for a little while...."

"Sure! I don't mind!

"Are you drunk?"

"Maybe, a little, but not enough to dull the senses. Just enough to enhance my experience here with you."

"Why do you always have to drink to be with me?"

"It's not about that at all. It's just how I carry out my day. I drink, I see you—"

"You're just always drunk when you're with me. It's like you *need* to be drunk to be with me."

"As I said, it's not like that, it's all about my need to always drink, regardless of what I'm doing."

Cleo shrugs. "Sorry, I guess I overthink things. I just had a really bad day. That creepy underwear guy was harassing me constantly about where his normal girl was, and I'm taking it out on you."

"I was actually meaning to talk to you about that. I thought about it, and I wanna do it."

"Sell your underwear?"

"Yeah, I can't find a job."

"Well, you are a lush."

"I-yam what I-yam."

"You're a goof tonight."

"I'm mentally unstable, I get weird highs."

"Okay, crazy lady."

"Just tell me, how do you do it?"

She scoots closer to me and sets her glass on the coffee table. She rolls her eyes and laughs at me. "You *really* wanna know?"

"Sure! I'm ready to take on this new experience." I punch the air a few times and wipe my nose like I'm an old-timey boxer. Cleo looks at me like I'm nuts.

"Cool your jets, fighter." Cleo takes a sip of her wine and waves her hands like this is all just too much for her. "Well, it's really easy, as I told you the first night. You just come into the bar, show him you're wearing the underwear by pulling the edge of your pants down slightly or, I guess, in your case, lifting up your skirt a little bit, then you go take them off in the bathroom. After that, you give it to him in a brown paper bag, he gives you fifty dollars. Badda-bing badda-boom. You're done."

"Then I just don't wear underwear the rest of the night?"

"No, dingus, you bring an extra pair in your purse."

I laugh hysterically and roll my eyes back at her. "This is all too easy, why doesn't everyone do it?" I smirk and twirl my fingers through my hair in a very flirtatious fashion.

"Some people have morals and shit."

"Whoa, whoa, whoa, morals? What's that?" I playfully shove her.

"Something weirdos and losers have." She shoves me back a little harder. I get up and jump on her lap, getting a small "oof" out of Cleo. She looks up at me with her pools of emeralds called eyes. I am dazzled and disorientated. I am drunk and dazed.

"Can you tell him that I want to sell my underwear?"

"Sure. Whatever you say, doll."

24

My dad used to call me Mushy. Ya know, the cute nickname from Michelle? I couldn't ever tell if he was being mean about my weight or just endearing. My ex heard my dad saying it once and he started calling me Mushy. I told this to Cleo in confidence, and she has decided that it was funny as hell. Now she calls me Mushy too. I hate this shit.

My mom has called me every day since I got here, and I have yet to respond. The phone is ringing now. The big letters glare at me, MOM. I finally answer. I am sober enough to deal with the headache ahead of me.

"Why haven't you been answering? Are you okay?"

"I'm fine, Mom."

"You don't sound fine. You sound strung out. Are you on pills again?"

"No, Mom. Just tired."

"So you haven't taken any pills?"

"No one is claiming I'm a saint."

"You need to take better care of yourself, sweetie. Especially because I'm not there to pick up the pieces."

"I know, I know. I'm trying, but it's just really hard."

"You're strong, I love you."

"I love you too, Mom. I'll talk to you tomorrow, okay?"

"Okay…. Chin up, bucko."

Then she was gone, and I was in a ball on the floor. That woman is too far away to stop me from crashing and burning. Did I do that on purpose? I scrape myself up and lie on the couch. I'm still in my pajamas and heavily debating on using my last five bucks to buy a gallon of ice cream and just eat it in my filth pile instead of going to the bar tonight. But that's fifty dollars I'd be wasting, and I can't afford to fuck it up. I peel my pajama bottoms off and then continue to lie in my own squalor. Then off comes the ragged top, and I'm in my underwear. I reach to the floor and grab my only pair of pants that fit, grungy jeans with holes all along the inner thighs. I pull them on and decide against finding a new shirt, pulling the same ratty one back on. I finally pull myself up and run for the door before I change my mind.

All of a sudden, I'm standing in front of the bar, staggering in the blinding sunlight. It's about four in the afternoon, and I'm ready. I head downstairs and am greeted by Cleo's knowing grin. She points to the corner where a grouchy old man is sitting. He is crouched over a table and is wearing a suit like he's straight from the south during the 1800s. I knew he was going to be strange, but strange is an understatement for this guy. I approach him and tap him on the shoulder. He turns gruffly and looks me up and down. I blush harshly and turn to look at Cleo for support. She is a busy bee at the bar on this hot day, and I'm left to my own devices. I turn back to this man that wants to jerk off in my underwear, and he is still staring at me.

"I want to sell you some stuff," I whisper hoarsely.

"You worn 'em for a whole day?"

"Twenty-four hours straight."

"You touch yourself in them? Get 'em wet?"

"Um…Yeah. A bunch." I do not remember Cleo telling me this part and I want to gag.

"Lemme see."

I hitch up my shirt and pull my belt loop down to reveal the band of my underwear.

"Not lacey enough, but I'll take 'em."

I pull my pants back up and rush to the bathroom. Slamming the door, I try to wiggle out of my underwear and jeans quickly, while not stumbling too much and while also not taking off my shoes and stepping on the disgusting bar toilet floor.

"FUCK," I grunt through gritted teeth. I finally pull my underwear off and throw it in one of the brown paper bags I bought in bulk. Now, just to slyly give the bag to him. I yank my clothes back on along with a fresh pair of underwear from my purse and creep over to his table to set it down. He looks at me and then swipes it, jamming it into his coat pocket. As I am about to walk away out of fear and embarrassment, he stuffs a fifty into my hand.

"Merry Christmas," he grumbles as he walks out of the Deaf Horse. I take residence up at the bar, and Cleo appears in front of me.

"How'd it go, little trooper?"

"Fine, I have no dignity left, pour me one."

"Shit, Michelle, you only have that fifty dollars to your name. Maybe we should go grocery shopping? I'm off in ten."

"Fine, but I'm buying wine at least. Two-buck-chuck never hurt a lady."

"I can get behind that." Cleo turns away from me and goes to cash out her drawer. I stare at other bar patrons, wondering if they know what I just did. How I just sold my dignity for barely anything. If they even cared. I am met with a resounding "no." Everyone is busy with their own lives and drinks. This is catastrophic for me. I wanted the attention of 'Oh my god, I can't believe you just did that.' Not even Cleo cares. I sigh a heavy sigh and put my weary head in my hands. Cleo returns. "Let's go, darling."

We leave the bar and go back into that intolerable sunlight. I wish I was something, anything. A painter, a writer, a singer—but I am nothing. Just a girl who sells her underwear.

I am laughing. I am laughing so hard, you'd think my gut would burst. Cleo's cart is full of things like kale and organic chicken.

"What the fuck am I supposed to do with that?" She sent me into the grocery store and told me that we were going to split up. I was going to fill my cart with what I thought I should get and Cleo was going to fill her cart with stuff she thought I should get. We met up as soon as we were done, and her cart is a laugh riot. I have no idea how to cook, and she grabbed all raw ingredients, things to cook stuff from scratch. Meanwhile, my cart is full of reasonable things like frozen dinners and chips, as well as a couple bottles of wine.

"Unacceptable. No wonder you feel gross all the time."

"You saying I'm gross?"

"NO, just saying you complain that you feel gross all the time and this is why."

"But I like these foods and I can't cook."

"I'll teach you to cook."

"Goddammit, Cleo."

"I'm making you a grown-up instead of a pithy little child." She grabs my cart and pushes it into a corner. "Employees can take care of that mess. It's what they get paid for anyway."

We push the cart full of fruit and vegetables up to the front registers and go to self-checkout because neither of us likes to be harassed. Well, not so much 'harassed' as 'bothered by people'. Everything adds up to $53.42. Cleo spots me the extra cash. We drag out bags full of food to her dumpy little Cabrio and hop inside. She adjusts all the mirrors lovingly and starts the car. Before I can even take a full drag of a cigarette, we are back at my apartment. This will be the first time ever that Cleo will get to see my rancid place. We march up the stairs and are greeted by my unhappy door hiding all my unhappy things. I open it, and Cleo immediately shrinks back in horror.

"What the absolute fuck, Michelle?!?"

There are piles and piles of clothing all over my small studio apartment. The bed is unkempt and the sink is full of dishes. Things are strewn everywhere in my tiny space. I guess you could say this was my version of unpacking.

"I told you it stank."

"No, you are the reason it stinks, my dear. Look at this place! Do you ever wash anything?"

"Sometimes. Maybe. Get off my dick, dude."

"I am not your *dude*. You've had my tongue down your throat." She goes over to my fridge and swings the door open. "What is all this?"

"Leftovers?"

"You gonna eat these leftovers?"

"…No."

Not even looking in my direction, Cleo extends her arm and flattens her palm. "Hand me a trash bag."

I reach under my leaking sink and hand her one. She starts taking things out of my fridge and dumping them into the bag. Once it's empty, she grabs the groceries and fills the fridge up again as I merely stand by in awe. She finishes and wipes her hands together, eyeing the rest of the place. Without a word, she sets to work, smelling the clothing on the floor, piece by piece, and either hanging them up in my closet or throwing them in my dirty clothes hamper. I am still speechless and immobile.

"Well, come on!" she yells from a pile. I clumsily stumble over to her and start helping the best way that I can. Shirt by shirt, dress by dress, we start getting somewhere. Soon, the pile is depleted, and I actually feel accomplished. This does not stop Cleo though, she just keeps moving on—the dishes, the vacuuming, the everything. I just submissively follow her and help where I can. Finally, she sits down.

"This place still smells." I wrinkle my nose.

"Goddammit, be grateful."

"I am grateful, sorry…. Thank you for helping me clean."

"Yeah, yeah. You're right though, this place stinks. Did a raccoon die in here or is it just your vag?"

"Jesus Christ, Cleo, it's not my vag."

"Let me smell." Cleo jumps on top of me and starts grabbing at my underwear. "Let me see those pretty pink lips."

"JESUS CHRIST. What are you doing? Where the fuck did this come from?"

"Come on, let's have sex," she breathes in my ear. "I'm tired of just making out. It's so boring. I just helped you, you help me." I try and wiggle out of her grasp, but she is holding on with strength that I can't fight after lying down for days on end. I start hyperventilating slightly. My breath is coming fast, and Cleo's hands keep wandering. She's kissing my neck, and I hate it. Why can't we just be friends? Why do we have to complicate things? I start slowly giving up as she pulls my pants down and my underwear off. My mind goes blank. All I can think is, *I wonder if birds think in chirps.*

I want to rip my skin off.

"Morning, darling."

I want to scream until my throat is raw.

"Want to go out for breakfast?"

I can't move or talk, and Cleo is staring at me. I roll over and face away from her.

"Feeling sick?"

I let out a grunt. All of a sudden, my insides are swimming. I get up and run for the bathroom. I throw everything inside of me up, which isn't much.

Cleo comes running in. "Darling, you okay?"

I wipe my mouth and look up at her. Cleo is pretty with long blonde hair and a round face. Her eyes are hazel and her lips are in a permanent pout. She is skinny, and I'm not. I hate her, but she is the only friend I've ever made that actually likes me. "I'm fine."

She helps me off the bathroom floor. She hugs me tightly and then lets go, putting her hands on my shoulders. "I adore you, Michelle."

"I adore you, Cleo," I say through pursed lips. I lean over and throw up again, barely making the toilet. It's all bile now. Cleo laughs like a tinkling bell. Goddammit, I hate her. I hate her. I hate her. I hate her.

"I think you're throwing up because of all the junk you were eating. Let me take you out for breakfast."

I'm still in my clothes from yesterday. I choose to not change and just push past her to grab my purse. We walk out the front door and I zone out for a minute looking at the bed.

"Come on, space cadet."

I close the door. I'm pretty sure birds think in chirps.

It's Thursday night, and we are at Fern's bar. Taking a break from the Deaf Horse's ten-dollar cocktails and sticking to three-fifty beers that taste like donkey piss. It's karaoke night, and Cleo is on fire. She's up, singing her third song of the night, "The Roof Is On Fire" by Bloodhound Gang. I'm singing along from the booth in the corner and raising my beer to her, my face plastered with a fake smile. I keep having flashbacks to that night. The night Cleo did…whatever. It's been over a month now, and Cleo must have sensed I was upset. She buys me flowers almost every day and is always drunk on my couch asking me about sea otters and why they hold hands. Her lips are made of steel and her tongue is always cold from the wine.

Tonight she asked me if I loved her. I said yes because I didn't want to get further into a conversation. I told her I loved her as a friend, and she slunk back in embarrassment at her question.

I am now full of beer and mildly happy. It's easier to fake my love for her when I'm drunk, which I nearly always am.

She finishes her song and comes back to join me at the booth. She laughs and falls into me. "I am having the time of my life. Why don't we do karaoke more often?"

"Because karaoke sucks. And my voice is terrible."

"Don't be a downer, go up and sing! Sing Fiona Apple the way you do for me at home. Pleeeeease?"

I look into those eyes of hers and all I see is her black soul. I am not coerced but I get up to fill a paper out anyway.

"YAY, GO MICHELLE!" she yells after me.

I go up to the karaoke table and write *Criminal- Fiona Apple* on a piece of paper. I smile as warmly as I can muster at the man working the table. He smiles back and winks, typing in my selection. I am not up for a while so I go outside for a cigarette. It's cold out and humid. I start feeling sticky and light one up. Across the parking lot, a truck pulls up. It's old and tattered, looking like it's about to fall apart any second. A tall, bearded man steps out of it. He looks at me and then turns back to the truck to lock the door. My heart starts to beat faster. If I had a type, this man would be it. Cleo comes crashing out of the bar door behind me.

"I'm so excited you're going—BYRON?!" She starts running towards the bearded man. Byron. She throws her arms around his bear shoulders and gives out a high-pitched squeal. I am trying to control my grinding teeth. Byron walks toward the bar door with Cleo in tow. "I can't believe you're here! I haven't seen you since college! Meet my friend, Michelle."

Byron looks me up and down and then extends his hand. He didn't look me up and down sexually though, more like he was checking to see if I was worth acknowledging. I take his hand and shake it.

"Hi."

"Nice to meet you…Michelle."

I feel like meat. Like a bag of meat. I choke on my breath for a second and then put out my cigarette. From inside, I hear my name. Shit. This is surely not going to impress him. He seems too cool for karaoke. Shit, shit, shit. I go inside and walk through the cornucopia of bad decisions. I grab the microphone and try to stop from shaking. Byron is at the bar, immediately grabbing the attention from the beautiful woman of a bartender that is always working karaoke night. She never pays attention to anyone, but Byron is a sexy hipster guy and sure to tip her just for the amount of tattooed cleavage she's showing off. The song starts and my smooth but flat voice caresses everyone's ears. Cleo is back sitting at our booth screaming at me in "woo"s. I watch as Byron takes his drink to our table. My voice starts to shake. Completely ignoring me, he is trying to talk to Cleo, who only pays attention to me in turn. The song finally finishes, and I scurry back to our booth. Cleo welcomes me with a giant hug and a kiss on the cheek while I'm sure I'm not masking my displeasure with it well, holding my arms to my side stiffly. Byron raises his eyebrow at me and takes a swig of his drink. Cleo signals me to go smoke and I grab my cigarettes. We start to walk for the bar door. Before Byron can follow us, she grabs me and pulls me outside.

"That guy is a dick."

"Byron?"

"He's a Darth Vader of a dick."

"What??"

"Forget it, that guy is the fucking worst."

"Why are you being so nice to him?"

"I'm just a nice girl, okay?"

I scoff in my head as Byron comes through the door.

"You ladies sure like to smoke."

"Oh, Byron. Please tell me how you've been, I couldn't hear inside."

"I've been fine. Been in Paris for a few months now."

"Wow, that's just sooo bourgeois."

"How've you been, Cleo, you little vixen."

"I'm a lesbian now."

"So, Michelle, you drunk?"

I choke again on my breath and this causes me to burp.

"So, yes."

"I have to go to the bathroom," I blurt before running inside. I slam the bathroom door behind me and let out a sob. I'm so fucking emotional right now. There's a knock on the door. I hear a muffled voice and yell "I'LL BE A MINUTE." The knocking persists and I swing the door open, ready to be snottier than usual to whoever is on the other side of it. It's Byron. He pushes me back inside and closes the door behind him.

"You wanna fuck?"

"Abso-fucking-lutely. Although I've never fucked standing up. Or in a bathroom. Ha…Ha. How are we gonna do this?"

Byron's mouth squishes the words out of me and the force of his body against mine nearly knocks the wind out of me. I am a slave to Byron now, putting my hands where he places them and fumbling to get my underwear off. He lifts me up on the sink and because of his tremendous height he easily slides his dick inside of me. As hard as I try, he won't kiss me during the actual sex. I feel like a little kid trying to climb up a mom's leg when she won't pick them up. Every thrust, my back thumps against the faucet, which is the most painful thing ever but I don't care. This is exactly what I've wanted since I got here. A good dicking. The physical pain numbs the emotional pain in my head, and while I'm being pounded by this stranger, I feel temporarily free. As Byron climaxes, he finally kisses me again, but only briefly before he pulls out and drips his seed onto the bathroom floor. I'm sure grosser things are down there anyway. He pulls his pants back up and walks through the bathroom door. I am floored. California is weird. I flounder to get my underwear back on and wash my hands in the sink. His semen is dripping down my leg, and I wipe it off with a paper towel. Exiting the bathroom, I take a deep breath, expecting the stares I never got at the Deaf Horse when I sold my underwear. No one is giving me a second glance. This time, I am grateful. I creep back to the booth and am glad to see Cleo for once in a long while, forgetting my hatred for just a moment, but Cleo does not seem too pleased to see me.

"What just happened?"

"I went to the bathroom."

"Byron went in after you."

"Yeah."

Cleo crosses her arms and refuses to look me in the eyes. "You guys fucked, didn't you?"

"Maybe, a little."

Cleo wriggles out of the booth. "Find your own way home." She walks away from me, looking back to see if I'll follow her. I don't, and this makes her even angrier. She is on the verge of a tantrum as Byron comes back with a fresh drink.

"Where's she going?"

"Home. Can you take me home?"

"Maybe."

We sit in silence as Cleo huffs away and Byron downs his drink.

"Wanna fuck again at my place?"

"Yeah."

We get up and start for the door. I brush my fingers against Byron's in hopes that he might hold my hand. It's a negative, Ghostrider. I curse myself for the attempt and follow Byron like a sheep through the door and into his car, desperate to feel numb again as the pain comes flooding back. He turns on the radio insanely loud so I don't even have an opportunity to talk. The car gets thrown in reverse and away we go. Through the black heart of Long Beach and beyond.

I wake up covered in sweat. Byron refused to leave the window open over-night for fear of 'street trolls'. That's what he calls homeless people. His closet is full of flannels and button-ups. He plays guitar and is in a band right now, but it's 'probably going nowhere but whatever and stuff.' I sit up and my fat roll pisses me off. I want to be sexy right now but there are no two ways about it. I'm repulsive. Thankfully, Byron is asleep and can't see this, so I climb over him and start putting on my clothes. I try to determine how good of an idea it is to wake him up and ask for a ride. Luckily, he starts to stir as I'm going through my inner monologue of what to say to make him not angry at being awoken.

"You're still here?" He mumbles through the sheets.

"I was just getting ready to go. I live a couple blocks away, if you wanna drop me off."

"Eh, I already have a good parking spot and I'm tired. If it's only a couple blocks then walk home. You could use it."

I start to tremble and it shows in my voice. "Okay. Do you wanna give me your number?"

"Sure. Three one zero five six three nine eight one seven."

I hastily write it on the back of my hand using a pen from his dresser. I then grab my jacket and shoes and creep out the door, as he has seemingly just fallen back asleep. It's got to be around eleven. I check my phone as I put my shoes on at his doorstep, and it is eleven-thirty. I decide to stop by Cleo's and see if she is in the mood for apologies.

A cigarette later and I'm at her doorstep. I knock my trademark knock and await the torrent of screaming. Cleo opens the door slowly and reveals a face streaked with tears.

"What the fuck are you doing here?"

"I came over to say I'm sorry I ditched you to have sex last night."

"I'm upset for far more reasons than that."

"I'm sorry because…he was a dick?"

"No. So far off."

"Why the hell are you upset then?!"

"Because I love you, I fucking love you!"

"What?! WHAT?!" I push through the door and into Cleo's apartment, slamming the door behind me. "I am not in love with you and I've told you that."

"You said you loved me!"

"As a friend! We aren't dating or anything Cleo, I can fuck everyone if I want to." All my anger and hatred comes rushing out of me all at once. I want to punch something.

"I thought maybe you'd come around to it!"

"Well, I wasn't going to! I like dick! DICK DICK DICK!"

"Then why'd you let me fuck you?!"

"I DIDN'T. YOU CHOSE THAT."

There is silence. So thick you could cut it. Cleo looks at me horrified and then buries her head in her hands, sobbing uncontrollably. I stand, staring at her, seething.

"I don't know what to say." Cleo lifts her head up.

"I'm sorry, that would be a good start! Then maybe, I'll never do it again! I JUST WANTED A FRIEND! That's all I wanted and you had to push me and push me to be more! I DON'T WANNA BE MORE."

"I didn't do anything wrong."

I back up until my back hits the door. I quietly open it and step outside. I am gone.

It was a rain-drenched night during my angsty sophomore year of high school, and I was busy instant messaging my friends on my crummy, hand-me-down laptop. My mom was away at a conference for some boring science thingy, and my dad was upstairs in the bedroom probably laughing at Family Guy. The internet went out, and I grumbled in distaste at the fact I had to go interact with my father on this rare occasion to get him to reset it. I huffed all the way up the stairs and knocked on his bedroom door. I heard some awful groaning that sounded like a cow being slaughtered.

"Uh, Dad, you okay?" I opened the door and was immediately met with the sight of a woman in the nude, riding my father like it was going out of style. I gasped and slammed the door. Immediately, I burst into tears and ran back to my room, slamming my door even harder, knocking it slightly off its hinges. My mom is a wonderful woman, and this fucking monster man that wears cargo shorts is humping some other monster dump. It's going to devastate her. My dad runs in after me, draped in a sheet, and throws his hands up.

"Please don't tell your mother."

"WHY THE FUCK SHOULDN'T I?!"

"I'll do anything if you don't tell your mother. I'll give you a thousand dollars if you just don't tell your mother."

"That's fucking stupid! I'm still telling Mom!"

"Ten thousand, right now. Well, tomorrow when the bank opens but please, whatever you do, don't tell your mother."

"What!? I...I don't know..."

"Please, Mushy. Please."

"But—But Mom..."

My dad looks at me with pleading eyes, and I just imagine the hurt on my mom's face. "Okay."

My dad walks over and hugs me, hugs me so tight I'd think he's trying to strangle the secret out of me. He lets go. "Just remember, Mushy, sweetie, I didn't do anything wrong."

My mother never knew where I got the money and she never asked. Maybe she didn't want to know. No one ever asks. I think everyone assumes that I either saved up or was a trust fund baby. People who know me better thought I got it when my dad died. It is my secret that I'll take to the grave. Years and years of bribe money that I spent willy-nilly. Maybe my mother asked my father where all his money was going to. Maybe my mother put it together that the money was disappearing from their bank accounts and I was somehow spending an insane amount on garbage kids don't need. I'll never know.

My mom calls in the morning. I tell her about Byron and how cute he is. She's excited for me. I get so sick with guilt. I want to take it all back but with my father being a rotting corpse, it's kinda hard.

I don't tell my mother how I have been making money though. Once again, she doesn't ask and probably doesn't want to know. I have been continuously selling my underwear to the patron from Deaf Horse, but now with Cleo and me out of sorts, I have to go bigger.

I'm on Craigslist with the blank 'for sale' ad up. What do I even write? I type DIRTY PANTIES FOR SALE. Shudder. GIRL SELLING DIRTY PANTIES. WILL MEET IN PERSON, IN PUBLIC PLACE. SERIOUS BUYERS ONLY. I use all caps to grab people's attention, like I'm screaming in their face about my gross underwear. I press save and post it with a picture of my ass that I took in an awkward pose I had no business being in. Ugh. I feel disgusting. I created a fake email and name to go along with the post. Within minutes, I have my first reply.

Will you do other things for money?

I respond with a resounding NO.

This is gonna be a long day. Most of these pervs are going to assume I'm a hooker. I was warned by the online forums that most of the other half will not show up. They just want someone to talk to. These sad, sad, terrible people just want some human contact and they think they can get it from me.

I get my second response: Want that pussay.

I decide to make a cup of coffee. I go over to my cupboard and grab a mug. I spoon in some Folgers crystals and then turn my sink on hot. As soon as the water hurts to the touch, I fill my mug up and stir it with the spoon. I return to my computer and find another response. This one seems serious, so I respond back and then lie down on my couch, falling down the rabbit hole of Pinterest.

The rest of the night goes by with a few more responses, all seemingly going nowhere until I get this in my inbox: Can you meet right now? I sit up abruptly and almost spill what remains of my cold coffee onto my lap. Yes, at the Starbucks on Long Beach Blvd. A few minutes go by and it seems like a decade. Finally, I get an answer. See you in 15 minutes, I'll be wearing yellow. Without delay, I throw my coat on and walk out the door.

Fifteen minutes later, I am standing under the Starbucks sign. Puffing heavily on a cigarette, eyeing the crowd. Who could he be? What does he look like? Is he old? Is he young? I see an old man with a yellow shirt. I hastily approach him and tap his shoulder. He looks at me in disgust and says in a flat tone, "You know smoking can kill you." I feel a hand on my shoulder. It is another man in a yellow shirt. He is young and, frankly, beautiful in a strangely attractive way. He has large eyes and mousy-brown hair that curls in different directions. His lips are pillowy, and I wanna kiss them until they bruise but in a totally NOT creepy way. His body is skinny but looks like there are muscles hidden underneath that yellow shirt, and he is very, very tall. I immediately swoon. Looking down at me, he smiles slightly. A very mischievous smile paints his lovely lips and he puts a fifty in my hand. I am wordless as he grabs the brown paper bag I am holding tightly to my chest and walks away without a word. I am trembling again. Shaking like a dumb, stupid leaf. He was probably so disappointed that I was the girl. He probably thought I was ugly. He most likely hates me. These are all the thoughts and more that come rushing through my head.

"Wowee," I say in a low tone to no one in particular.

Byron hasn't returned my call, and it's been three days. Isn't that the guy waiting period? Three days? I had heard that somewhere and today is the third day. I am pacing my apartment, not even thinking about the Cleo situation. Not even dreaming of thinking about the mystery of where I got my money. Totally not even thinking about these things at all. Not worried about Byron, not worried about everything. I am impenetrable. I have no friends again, no lover. I start throwing a pity party for myself as the phone rings. I stop dead in my tracks. Could it be? I scurry to my phone and it is. Oh, joyous day. I am a genius. I dance a little as I answer my phone, but only after five rings. I don't want to seem desperate.

"Hello?" I answer timidly

"Hey. What are you doing?"

"Oh, I was just about to go to the bar with a couple friends," I say, looking down at my pajamas that are still on. Such lies, such devious little lies.

"Wanna fuck?"

"I was actually thinking we could go to the bar first and have some drinks. Maybe even dinner?"

"No. I think screwing is a hundred percent okay without that."

"Oh. So. Just sex."

"Listen, Megan. Let's fuck, okay? Come over."

"My name is Michelle." I grate my teeth.

"Sure…Michelle. Wear something sexy."

I am greeted with the *BEEP BEEP* of being hung up on. I throw down the phone and continue pacing. Just wanna fuck, huh? I'll wear something so sexy that he'll *have* to go on a date with me. He'll be so in love that his heart will jump out of his chest. I am such a fucking moron. I dive into the bathroom and dig through my unused makeup bag. I apply a thick coat of foundation and then use an eyebrow pencil to make my eyebrows darker. This is also to hide the fact that I never pluck my eyebrows. Then, I slick on some liquid eyeliner and mascara. My eyes start to pop, and with a little blush, so do my cheeks. I run to the closet and pick out my little black dress and when I say little, I mean hooker little. It's made of lace and rides up so high my ass peeks out every few steps.

The walk to Byron's is smooth and easy. I smoke my cigarette and feel incredibly sensual. I puff each puff as if I was Marilyn Monroe herself. This trip builds my confidence with each step. I arrive at Byron's and rap on the door. I hear awful groans like a cow being slaughtered. I never learn.

"Byron, you okay?" I open the door. I am greeted with the naked ass of a woman riding Byron like it's going out of style. He knocks her off and looks at me in surprise.

"You're a bigger girl, I thought the walk would take longer."

"Are you fucking kidding me?"

"Michelle, meet Megan."

The blonde that is skinny as a rail looks at me with a grin. "Nice to meet you, sorry I took so long."

"I'm not doing this, no fucking way."

"What's wrong? Why don't you come join in?"

"I'm not gonna be a part of your fuck party! I just wanted to go on a date with you."

"I wanna have some fun, nothing serious. I am a man of the people, I can't get tied down or attached. I belong to everybody. I just wanna fuck some people. Don't you feel lucky that you're one of them?"

"LUCKY?! LUCKY!!"

I slam the door behind me.

I've never been good with sex. I lost my virginity to a boy named Dylan. He was sweet enough and pretty much beyond perfect. He told me I was beautiful and that curvy girls were sexy as hell. I was in love. His hair curled and so did his lips when he saw me. One day, he just stopped loving me. He told me he didn't trust women because of his mother doing meth or whatever drug she was into. I didn't ask because I knew he wouldn't answer. I was clingy and ruined everything. I'll never forgive myself for that. The only other boy I slept with was my infamous ex. I don't like talking about him though.

I check my email. Thirty responses. I sip my coffee carefully and check the first one. Nothing, just a guy asking for sex. The next one warrants a spit take but I don't do one because those never happen in real life. I'm not a fucking cartoon. It's a picture of a giant erect penis that just says I can B ur birthday boy. Yuck. Delete. What does that even mean? As I am searching through the messages for my bread and butter, I see that secret sexy guy sent me another email.

Your scent is intoxicating. Please meet me again. I squeal with joy. Who cares that this is an anonymous creep who just cares about my animalistic scent? He is beautiful, and I want to have his babies. I respond as quickly as my fingers can type, Yes, when would you like to meet?

As soon as I can take another sip of coffee, he responds, Right now, same place.

My feet cannot take me there quick enough. I arrive in only ten minutes and decide to get a large iced coffee. The barista eyes me, and I can't tell if it's because of my hurriedly applied makeup or because he knows I sell underwear here. I have returned five times since my first encounter with the sexy man. Two of the times, someone actually showed up. Most of the time, I just sit in the corner and try to hold in the sobs as I contemplate my life, iced coffee in hand. At least I buy shit, you judgemental barista prick.

I hear the tinkling of the bell that alerts employees that someone has arrived. I turn without a single ounce of grace and see my yellow-shirted man. He approaches me and smiles his mischievous smile again.

"Getting some coffee?"

"Yes."

"Would you like me to join you?"

"Sure."

Everything inside of me is screaming that this is a bad idea. Getting coffee with a guy I sell my private garments to? My mother would have a coronary. My dad is probably rolling over in his grave right now. Then again, he's probably been eternally spinning since he died from all the dumb shit I do.

He orders his coffee and turns to me again. "What is your real name? I know Kitty isn't it."

"I can't reveal that information. I don't know if you are a serial killer or some kind of crazy guy."

"Well, my name is Marly. But you can call me Mar. And I promise that I don't kill people or anything like that. Will you at least tell me why you picked the name Kitty?"

"It sounded like a good name for a girl who sells her underwear."

The barista gives me a look as he's preparing Mar's coffee. I'm past the point of shame. Shame is for goobers and squares. I'm enlightened, I sell my underwear. I'm special.

"You sure are something. And very beautiful too."

"No, I'm just fat and gross."

"If you say so."

I laugh Cleo's tinkly bell laugh that seems so appealing, and we take our coffees to a small table outside. I light up a cigarette and offer the pack to Mar. He shakes his head and frowns.

"Those kill you, you know."

"I've been smoking for five years. I don't plan on stopping because some guy I sell my underwear to says it's bad for me."

"You are basing this whole interaction around the fact that I'm a customer and you're the proprietor. This can be more than that, you know."

"More? How so?"

"I can help you. I know a lot about this…industry."

"What information do you have for me, Captain?"

I salute him and he laughs a tiny bit.

"Have you thought about selling other services?"

"Oh my flippin' God, I am not a prostitute. Jesus."

"No, not like sex, like stories of what you do in your underwear, bras, tights, shoes…stuff like that. Even conversation should cost the customer."

"Are you fucking serious?"

"Yeah, you can sell a lot. Just be careful."

"Yeah, yeah, I'm careful."

"You're having coffee with a stranger, you're not very careful."

"Hey, it's in public and you're not dangerous, you even said so."

"And you trust me?" He scoots his chair closer and looks me square in the eyes. "You're not scared of me?"

"No, you're harmless like a little sheep."

"Oh yeah?" I laugh at him and he grabs my hand. This makes me recoil involuntarily, and he frowns again.

"Don't you like me?"

"I—I don't know. You're very attractive, but…I sell you my underwear."

"You know, I'm a human being too."

He stands up and walks away.

Mar's advice was invaluable. I've been raking in the dough. Selling everything I could possibly think of. I even sold all my old clothing that didn't fit from when I was skinny for a year. Because of the selling of stories and conversation time, I have a pretty consistent new client under the alias of John. Real original, I know. He asked me yesterday for a 'Big Adventure Story', so I made up some crap about how I did ecstasy and got fucked in a bathroom. He totally ate it up, and that was another eighty dollars in my pocket. The next time we met, he asked if he could buy me panties and then buy them back from me after I wore them. I okayed this and reveled in the idea of being treated like an underwear princess.

Today I received another email from Mar. He apologized for walking out on me and asked if he could have another chance to prove that he was not a weirdo. I agreed to it, and we are meeting tonight. I am dressing to the nines and meeting him at a restaurant downtown called the Potholder. It's mainly a breakfast place, but they have good burgers too. As I'm walking there, I feel giddy. Mar is a beautiful man, and I would love to date him but…I can't get past the selling my underwear to him thing. What kind of perv buys women's underwear? And if we dated, would just *my* underwear be enough? Would he still buy other women's underwear? There are so many questions buzzing through my mind, but I have arrived, and it's time to charm the pants off this immoral man.

He already has a booth and waves me over.

"Hi, Kitty. Nice to see you."

"Hey, Mar. You can, uh, call me Michelle now."

"Okay, Michelle it is. Much better than Kitty, in my opinion."

I sit down and brush the stray hairs from my face. I feel extra fat tonight and I hope it doesn't show. I am wearing my little black dress that didn't get any use from my last encounter with a boy. Stupid Byron, I hope his dick rots off.

"You look lovely."

"Thank you very much. How have you been? Buying more ladies' underwear?"

"No. Your panties are the only ones I'm interested in."

The waitress comes over and stands in front of our table. She seems bored beyond belief and is chewing a wad of gum the size of a baby's fist.

"What can I get you guys?"

"I'll have a porky burger and an iced tea." Mar smiles. He waves his hand at me. "And she'll be having…"

"Oh! I didn't even look at the menu! A porky burger will be fine as well, but I'd like mine plain, please, with a diet coke."

"Meat, cheese, and bun?" She pops her gum.

"Yes, ma'am."

The waitress departs, and Mar makes some pretty intense eye contact. The kind that makes you swear they can see right through your skull and into your brain. I start to feel very nervous and I can feel my ass sweat start sticking my skin to the faux leather booth.

"So… Do you like cats?" I look around nervously because looking directly at Mar is like looking at the sun. I'm tapping my fingers on the table, not sure what I'm doing with myself.

"Um, I had one growing up—"

"What do you do with my underwear?!?" I blurt out, looking at him out of the corner of my eye, which makes him snort unreasonably loud.

"Well, I use them when I jerk off. I either wrap them around my penis when I jerk off, smell them as I jerk off, or put them in my mouth. What did you think I did with them? Use them as window decoration?" This makes me snort equally loud and breaks some of the tension I felt at being in a diner with a self-proclaimed perv.

"No! But, like, why do you do that? What started all of this?"

"I don't know. I just like the scent of a woman, and also it feels humiliating. I like being humiliated. It gets me off."

I blush so hard that I can feel the heat. I am very flattered that he thinks I'm worthy of this weird fetish of his.

"Anything else that gets you off?"

"Hmmm…dinosaur roleplay, cartoon women, eating bananas slowly in front of homeless people…."

"Uh, *WHAT*?"

I am blushing so intensely I could swear that he could feel the heat radiating off of me from across the table.

"I am kidding. These are jokes. Ha ha, please laugh."

"You are a very funny man, Mr. Mar." I giggle a little too girlishly. He grabs my hand, and this time I don't pull away. "I'm sorry I treated you as less than a human being the other night. I am just having a hard time getting past the business aspect of our relationship and I really do like you. You seem sweet and nice, but I need to get to know you a little better before I do anything crazy."

"Crazy?"

"I don't know, maybe I'm already doing something crazy. We are kinda on a date thing."

"Well, what do you wanna know?"

"Everything. Tell me everything about you."

Our food shows up, and the waitress pops her gum at us again. "Enjoy," she drawls as she walks away without even looking at us. I immediately dig in as Mar looks on and grins.

"I am a marine biology major. I graduated last spring and I work at the aquarium."

"Wow, I would have never have guessed in a million years that you were into marine biology."

"I love animals. It's definitely my passion. I think they are far more interesting than people."

"People do suck a bunch."

"Why do you say that?"

"I've never been good at having friends. They always screw me over and treat me like crap." The words are flowing out of me so fast and I can't stop them. I just keep word-vomiting on this poor guy. Way to make myself unsexy. "I haven't really had boyfriends either. I had two, but they didn't work out."

"I'm sorry. I really am. I apologize for the human race."

I almost choke on my food. Mar laughs loudly.

"You okay there?"

"Yeah, just the whole apologizing for the human race thing has me in stitches over here."

"Do you want to know more about me?"

"Yes, please."

"My hobbies include camping, hiking, riding my bike anywhere, and drawing. I love to draw. I get these pictures in my head and I have to put them somewhere so I just transfer them to paper."

"We could not be more different. I love to laze around and do nothing."

"We can change that." He takes a bite of his burger and puts his hand over his mouth as he chews. Jeez, he's polite too?

"Anything else you want to tell me? Your social security number? Your mother's maiden name?" I finish my burger way too fast and sip on my diet coke, playing coy like I didn't just hork down my food. I raise an eyebrow.

"No, I think you'll get to know me over time."

"Over time? You plan on spending more time with me?"

"As much as you'll let me."

"You are too sweet to me."

"Something you have to learn, Michelle, is that you deserve being treated nicely. Everyone does."

I pause and ponder on this. I really don't think *everyone* deserves it. Mar finishes his burger and grabs my hand one last time.

"Wanna go on a walk?"

"I'd love to."

Mar throws some money on the table, and we depart onto the street. As we walk toward downtown, Mar kisses me on the cheek. Just one small peck that makes me feel like I'm about to collapse. My knees are made of goo and I am fluttering inside. I have never been treated so nicely in my life, except for maybe Dylan but fuck Dylan. Mar is Jesus compared to Dylan. I clamber for words, but nothing comes to me. Instead, we just walk in silence. But one of those nice silences where you're sure you're both just thinking pleasant thoughts.

John asked me to go get coffee with him. I told him it would cost one hundred dollars so he wouldn't want to go anymore, but he accepted the offer anyway. Part of me is joyful for the hundred dollars, but another part of me is in emotional agony at the thought of getting coffee with this slimeball. He wants to talk for hours and gets angry when I don't respond immediately.

I meet him at the same coffee shop I always go to for underwear selling, and we have some polite conversation. He keeps interjecting questions about my sex life, which I ignore and try to move away from. John shows me pictures of other girls he buys underwear from. This disturbs me in a number of ways, and I cut coffee short. I walk home, shaking, and call Mar.

"I don't want to do that ever again."

"Then you don't have to, sweet thing."

"It was so creepy."

"What are you doing right now?"

I look around my apartment. I have kept it clean and the refrigerator fully stocked since Cleo had helped me clean it the first time. There is a small pile of clothing at the foot of my bed and a bit of clutter on the coffee table, something that I was planning on remedying tonight. "Cleaning and then probably watching a movie."

"Can I join you?"

"Sure. I'll probably be done cleaning by the time you get here, but we can watch a movie together."

I hang up the phone and immediately take to the clothing pile, hanging up the items systematically with their brethren. I change into a sexier dress and then scoop the clutter off the table to disperse it into its proper locations. Right as I finish, I hear a knock at the door. I swing it open and there is Mar, holding a couple daffodils and smiling at me with a big toothy grin. I smile back and take the flowers.

"You really shouldn't have."

"But I did because you deserve it."

I dig under the sink and find the only thing that resembles a vase, a pot that I had bought with the intention of planting basil in it. I fill it with water and put the flowers in it, placing the pot on my kitchen counter.

"They are lovely. Thank you."

Mar puts his hand lovingly on the back of my neck and lightly presses it for me to turn towards him.

"Can I kiss you?"

"Maybe after some wine."

I hadn't drunk alcohol in a very long time. I had been too busy cleaning and doing grown-up things. It turns out, from my first experience cleaning alone, that cleaning drunk is very hard. I was sloppy and ended up spilling a bucket full of bleach onto the tile floor. It did cure the rot stink smell though, only to replace it with a bleachy smell. I guess it is preferable and way less embarrassing with a strange man in the house. I pull a bottle of wine from the fridge, the one I had bought with Cleo, and luckily, since it's the cheap kind, it just has a twist-off top. I pour two glasses and hand him one, which he raises to me before taking a sip and making a slightly disgusted face. I snort behind my hand.

"Sorry, it is cheap."

"Oh it's fine, I was expecting something from the French mountains aged about forty years, but I suppose this will do." He winks taking another sip, trying to hide his shudder of distaste. I feel unusually close to Mar even though we barely know each other.

"Wanna dig through my dirty clothes hamper?" I wink at Mar.

"Ha. You're a very funny lady. Do you think I would do something so disgusting? Because I totally will."

He puts down his wine glass and starts to tickle me. I shriek and almost spill my own wine. He snickers and goes in for more. I slap his hand and scream, "Stop it, you freak!"

"I'm a freak, huh? Would a freak do…this?!"

He tackles me to the floor and tickles me even harder. My wine spills everywhere, and I cackle loudly, writhing around trying to get out of his grasp.

"SERIOUSLY, YOU'RE HURTING ME!"

He stops abruptly and looks down at me. "Am I really?"

"…No…" I whisper.

This leads him to tickle me even harder. After a minute, we both get tired and he slumps over next to me. Breathing hard, we look at each other and grin. He puts his hand on my cheek and kisses me very gently.

What comes next is surprising, seeing as I barely know this guy. I roll on top of him and straddle his hips. He kisses my neck as I hike my dress up and grind down on him. Before I know it, we are far past the point of no return. I am exposed. He is exposed. But he isn't just touching my skin, he is feeling me. He isn't just kissing me, he is tasting me. And he isn't just looking at me, he is seeing me.

I wake up crying. I had another dream about Cleo. Cleo moving her hands all over me, Cleo destroying the trust I had in her. I am crying, and Mar is lying next to me. He reaches over and laces his fingers in my hair. I turn away from him in embarrassment and shield my face with my hands. I am revolting. He pulls me close and holds me while I cry. When I am done, he wipes the tears away from my cheeks and lightly kisses my forehead. Kindness makes me nervous. It makes me want to vomit.

I used to believe that I didn't deserve kindness. And I still kind of really do, but Mar shows so much. My mom always told me, 'You get loved the way you love yourself.' Which usually makes me feel like shit because I'm pretty self-loathing. But now I look back on those words and they fill me with joy because this man, this strange man, thinks I'm just the bee's knees. He treats me like a human being. Even more than that, he treats me like I mean something to him. I've never had that. I've always been discarded or treated like I was a skin-bag with some holes.

I nuzzle into him and we lay in sweet silence for a good half an hour. There is no need for words, and that's fine. He doesn't ask why I was crying, and I couldn't appreciate it more. Finally, he whispers in my ear, "I love you."

I sit straight up and huddle on one side of the bed, my heart pounding in my throat. "Love me? You don't even know me!"

"I love what I've seen and I couldn't be happier that you're mine."

"Yours? We aren't dating! I don't even know who you are!" My brain is running a hundred miles a minute. How can this be happening? I never asked for it to be THIS serious! Why do people keep pushing me into things I'm not comfortable with? First Cleo, now Mar.

"Why can't I just love you and let that be that? Why do you have to make it so complicated?"

"*I'm* making it complicated? HA." I get out of bed and start getting dressed in a huff. I'm officially pissed. "I don't know what you want me to say."

"Say you love me too."

"I don't know if I do yet! I have to get to know you."

"You know my deepest personal secret. That's not enough?"

I halt what I'm doing and stomp over to the bed where Mar is still lying down. I lean in as close as I can possibly get without touching him. "Not even a little bit." My rage is boiling just beneath the surface, ready to fight if need be.

"Well, I love you, and you won't get rid of me so easily."

"Fine. But—" I look him up and down and grimace. "—I'm not saying it back."

"Deal."

I huff over to my coffee pot and turn it on. I am so deliriously angry, I want to scream. No one falls in love that easily. This isn't some fucking '80s movie. I turn back to look at him to yell some more, and he is standing right behind me. He takes my hand and presses his forehead against mine. The anger in me subsides a little, and I sigh.

"I'm sorry. I just don't know how to be loved and also this is *really* sudden."

"It's okay. I don't know how to stop jerking off into women's underwear. We all have our things."

I laugh, just a little, and look into his eyes. "You have to be okay that I'm not ready to say something so drastic."

"I'll try."

John has been extra creepy lately. And by extra creepy, I mean the level of creepy that you'd expect out of John Wayne Gacy. I started getting really terrified and decided to cut all ties with him. I deleted my email account and changed my alias, pictures, and everything else. I was horrified. His last email stated, U R mine and Ill find U no matter wut.

Mar has been spending the night every night. He tells me he loves me every single day, without fail. I smile every time and say, "Thank you." This is it, nothing more, no false expectations, no lies. I couldn't lie to Mar, he's too sweet. He's like a big ol' puppy with paws too big for his body. He just stumbles around with a giant grin on his face like the world is perfect. To be so blind, ignorant, and delusional must be wonderful. We spend most of our time indoors, talking about our views on different things and arguing our points before deciding that we are both far too stubborn so we just watch TV. Sometimes we go out into the great unknown for sustenance or alcohol, but it's rare and far between. When we do go out, we hold hands and laugh like everything is fine and we are a happy couple, which for the most part, we are. But I can tell in Mar's eyes that he wants me to love him back, and sometimes it's a burden too big to carry. I think every day about breaking it off with him but I couldn't put him through so much pain and I like him too much to let go. He makes me feel like I exist. I am partly a selfish ass.

We are lying in my bed watching the movie *Rushmore*, because why not, and Mar rolls over to me, putting his head in my lap.

"Let's run away together."

"Run away? Where to?"

"I don't know, Hawaii?"

"Hawaii is really expensive. A gallon of milk is like eight dollars."

"Well, fine, where do *you* want to run away to?"

"Nowhere, I like it here. I have nothing to run away from. Except maybe John."

"Boo, you're no fun."

"Yeah, yeah, I'm the fun killer."

My phone vibrates, I have an email. I check it, and it's from John. It reads, I no U R kitty I would recognize dat ass anywhere. U better meet me 2 sell those panties bak to me. I spent 100 bucks on those.

I freeze. I can't believe it. Why won't this guy leave me alone? I am just some dumb kid, and it's just some dumb underwear.

"I've changed my mind. Let's run away."

"What's wrong, Mushy?"

"Don't call me Mushy, and nothing."

"Nothing my ass." He grabs for my phone and wrestles it away from me. "John, again? I thought you changed your email and everything."

"I did. I don't know how he found me."

"Well, you do have a distinctive ass."

"Shuddup!"

I grab my phone back and respond to John's message, Please leave me alone.

We lie back, and my heart beats out of my chest. I don't actually want him to respond, but the suspense is killing me. I kinda want him to respond so I can just know he got it. That he got the hint. That he will leave me alone. Some kind of confirmation would be nice. Mar leans over and looks at me long and hard. He furrows his brow and frowns.

"I'm worried."

"What about?"

"John, he could be dangerous."

"I'm sure he's just a harmless creep. Just wanting to scare me into selling him shit."

"Please stop selling your underwear, Michelle."

"What?!"

"I'm really worried. Please stop."

"How will I pay rent?"

"I'll help you, we could move in together and—"

"NO. I like living in my own apartment, thank you very much. I don't want your help, I just want to support myself."

"You could actually get a job."

"You're a jerk."

Mar sits up abruptly, almost toppling me over the edge of the bed. "Why??"

"Because I've been trying, it's not like I'm lazy!" That's a lie. I'm totally lazy, I haven't looked for a job in weeks, but he doesn't need to know that. He can live in a world where I have been job hunting religiously.

"Well, let's try harder, together."

"Fine. Fine! I'll stop."

"Now I get to have your underwear all to myself."

"Good for you."

My phone vibrates again, and I look at it inconspicuously as if I had just received a normal text message or a Facebook notification. It's John. Im cumming after U. I want my merchandise.

I slam my phone down and stare at the television screen.

"What, babe?"

"Just deleted my email and shit. No big deal."

"Oh, cool."

We huddle together and watch the movie. We don't speak again until the next morning.

I have been selling my underwear without Mar knowing for two weeks. Luckily, I have continuously changed my email and stopped adding butt pictures to my ads so it's harder for John to track me. Unluckily, I get a threatening email every few days and have to change it again. I feel really bad about it, but what Mar doesn't know won't hurt him.

My mom called. She's coming to visit this week, and I could not be happier. She wants to see my new place and to see all the sights in Long Beach. I told her it's a dump, but she won't listen. She thinks my life is some amazing heap of success. She has no idea what I have waiting for her. A failure of a daughter that sells her underwear and had sex with one of her clients. My stomach loops in knots every time I think about the possibility of her finding out.

I've been in top-notch cleaning mode, and it's turning out not too shabby. My mother shouldn't be horrified. Maybe just mildly disappointed. My apartment smells like bleach still and everything is perfectly organized. I've even taken up knitting to show my mom that I have hobbies and actually do something.

Mar comes over to help me clean and notices my pile of yarn.

"What are you, Martha Stewart now?"

"I just like to knit, okay? That isn't weird or anything."

"It's totally weird, you've never done anything like it."

"It's to impress my mom."

"How will that impress your mom?"

"She'll think I *do* something."

Mar starts picking up my few items of clothing on the floor and tosses them in the dirty clothes hamper.

"Did you start filling out those applications I got you?"

"No, I've been busy cleaning."

"I'll clean, just fill out the applications."

I grumble to myself and grab the stack and a pen. My only previous work experience was assembling sandwiches at a Subway for two months, no one's gonna hire my experience-less ass. I start scrawling my basic information on the Starbucks application. They will *definitely* never hire me. At least the one I sell my underwear at won't.

"Starbucks? Really, Mar?"

"Just turn it in at the one on Bellflower."

"I don't have a car, how am I gonna get to these places?"

"The bus."

"I hate the bus."

"Then I'll drive you. Just stop complaining for like two minutes."

Mar sure is grumpy today. He gets grumpier every day that I don't say the magic words that will somehow make our relationship special. He just pouts and takes digs at me every opportunity that he can. I want to keep liking him because he is very sweet to me, but it is hard when he is being such a whiny baby.

Mar is cleaning my stove, and I'm really dilly-dallying on these applications. I keep hemming and hawing over them and asking weird questions like, "Do you think birds think in chirps?"

"I don't know, Michelle. I don't think they think at all."

"Maybe they do.... I think they do."

"Stop procrastinating."

I flip through the rest of the applications and start to get flustered and overwhelmed.

"I'm not filling these out right now."

"Why not? You need a job, Mushy." I flinch at the use of my least favorite nickname.

"I don't want to do this. This is too much work."

"You have to put some effort into finding a job. They don't just fall into your lap."

I start crying quietly. I feel trapped. I feel so trapped in my stupid life. I sell underwear, I practically live with this boy, and my mom is gonna be here in three days to judge the way I live. What am I gonna do when she asks me to show her where I work? Then, to top this all off, my phone goes off, alerting me that John has found me yet again.

Plz just let me buy the merchandise off U. just meet me 1 more time. Ill give U 80 for each pair.

I sob hysterically, like a psycho person. Mar looks over at me, absolutely stunned.

"Babe, what's going on?" He walks over to me and wraps me in his arms. I feel so bad for what I'm about to say.

"I have to meet John one last time."

"What the fuck are you talking about?" He backs away from me and raises his eyebrows.

"He found me. I've still been selling my underwear, and he found me." Each word comes out with a sob, and I sound like I'm insane.

He grabs both of my shoulders, "YOU'VE STILL BEEN SELLING YOUR UNDERWEAR?! And you want to MEET JOHN AGAIN?!"

"He's offering me eighty dollars a pair."

"At least tell him I'll meet him to get the money. You're not going, and that's final. This guy is dangerous, Michelle."

"Okay, okay." I start to calm down a little. "Are you mad at me?"

"Yes. But if you're not going to listen to me and do it anyway, I want you to at least be safe."

I type out, I won't meet you but my friend will. He can meet you at the Starbucks over on Long Beach Boulevard.

I catch Mar looking over my shoulder. "Friend?"

"I don't want to explain to this gross-ass the complexities of our relationship."

"Uh huh."

My phone vibrates. Tell UR friend not to bring a knife 2 a gunfight. I cant guarantee his safety.

Mar looks at me and then lets out an angry growl. "I'm not fucking going, you're not fucking going, it's over."

I start crying again, and this time I just let it all out. I told you, I never cry and now I'm a big fucking blubbering baby, crying all the time. I open my laptop and actually delete my email and delete the craigslist post for real. I can't live like this anymore. I need a real job.

I turn in my applications with the help of Mar. We went all over the city since I am desperate for anything. I applied to almost every business I possibly could downtown because at least some of them sounded fun. They have an arcade, a movie theater, a comedy club, etc. He drives me all over Long Beach and wastes a ton of gas, but he knows my money is tight with the not selling underwear thing going on. Mar was really mad the first day he found out, and I regretted even telling him. It felt like things were going to go south. The second day he let me cuddle him a bit reluctantly. Now, it being the third day, he has forgiven me and let it go. At least that's what he told me. Who knows if this is just a new rage for him to harbor against me. Something that he can use to manipulate me, but the logical side of my brain says not everyone in my life is like that.

We turn down Magnolia, and we are now heading home. Back to the old studio apartment. He wants to order Indian food for dinner and watch *The Darjeeling Limited* as a reward for me getting my shit together. I agreed to this even though he made several faces that triggered my moments of panic because I'm terrified Mar is going to turn out like everyone else. Like, when is the other shoe going to drop?

We park pretty far away from the apartment because of how packed the streets are tonight and go inside. He holds my hand but very limp like a dead fish as if he's saying, *I don't give a shit about you anymore, Michelle.* The paranoia is real tonight. I feel like I'm drowning in it.

While we wait for the food to show up, we sit on the balcony, wallowing in our discomfort, and share a cigarette. He grumbles the whole time because he says I should quit. Another notch on the complaining pole. As if he wasn't even sharing it with me. It feels like he doesn't really like me for me. He's acting like a child, trying to change me as if I was made of Playdough and could be molded into the girlfriend he wants. I'll never be the girlfriend of his dreams, and he makes it a little too clear.

My mom is arriving in the morning. I've been feeling pangs of gnawing guilt in the back of my head to tell my mother about the money from dad, but I wouldn't even know how. What if she doesn't love me anymore? I am a pity party, floating through my own life.

"Want to get drunk?" I look at Mar and raise my eyebrows up and down in a goofy way.

Mar passes me back the cigarette and furrows his brow. "No."

"Why not? I've got some wine, and it'll be fun," I whine in my cute little voice that I know he can't resist.

"When you get drunk, you get too sloppy. I feel bad having sex with you when you're drunk."

"What if I don't want to have sex?" I take another drag on the cigarette and blow it into Mar's face.

He coughs. "Well, I just don't want to."

"Well, I'm going to."

"Then I'll just leave."

"Leave then, you big baby. It's okay to drink sometimes. I don't do it every day anymore. It's all about control and rationing."

"Fine, I'll stay, but no sex."

"Fine then!" I slam my hands down on my thighs and jump to my feet. I'm getting really sick of his attitude.

I step inside the apartment, still smoking my cigarette. I don't care, the bleach smell will cover it up anyway. I grab a bottle of wine and twist off the little metal cap. I go back out onto the balcony and take a long swig while standing in the doorway, making sure he gets a good look at me while I do it. Mar crosses his arms and huffs some retort that I'm sure is awful, but he's so quiet that I can't hear it.

"What did you say?"

"Alcohol makes you gain weight."

"What-fucking-ever." I feel like smashing this bottle over his damn head. Like I really needed the guilt trip.

I take another drink with my back turned to him and finish my cigarette. The doorbell rings, and I go to answer the door, bottle in hand. Who cares who sees this tragedy play out?

"Delivery for Michelle?"

"Speaking to her."

I take the food and hand him some worn five-dollar bills. He takes them and departs from my doorstep. I slam the door aggressively so the great party pooper on the balcony can hear it and pop the movie in. Mar is still sitting out there, just getting angrier and angrier. I open up the food and take huge bites of it. If I'm gonna be fat, then oh well. At least I get to eat and drink what I want. I'm over people making me feel bad about myself because I am simply living my life. The opening of the movie has me engrossed, and I feel Mar enter the apartment. He sits next to me and pauses the movie. I look up at him, and he looks like a dog that has been drowned. He starts shuddering like he's holding back tears.

"I'm sorry I've been so cruel."

"Yeah, it's not okay." I put the food in my hands down and turn to face him, lips pursed, waiting for him to continue.

He puts his hand on mine and starts tearing up. "I'm just a big jerk."

"Well knock it off then and have some wine." I grab for the remote to turn the movie back on, and he pushes my hand back.

"I'm trying to apologize, stop being so rude." His eyes squint hard at me.

I put my hands up as if suggesting that I'm surrendering. "I'm listening."

"I just really love you and I want to make it work. Even though you don't love me."

I hesitate and catch my words in my throat. I'm trying to be delicate. Should I say it? Should I just do it to make him happy? *Do I love him?*

"You shouldn't say things like that." Tears well up in my eyes, and I look to the ceiling to calm my tear ducts and catch the drops before they fall.

"That you don't love me?"

"Yes." I continue to stare upwards with the hopes that he won't make eye contact with me so I won't cry.

"Why, Michelle?"

I sigh heavily since he is really going to make me say it. "Because maybe I do. I don't know. I've never really loved anyone before. Just maybe if you stopped pressuring me to feel it, I could figure it out." I finally cast my eyes in his direction, looking for a response. Looking for some kind of empathy.

Mar gets really quiet looking down at the floor and then lifts his head up to kiss me lightly. Then he pats me on the head and presses the play button on the remote. I just stare at him as he grabs his food and digs in. I don't know what else to say or do. I am dumbfounded. This man is truly insane.

My mom arrives safe and sound, and when Mar and I pick her up at the airport, she hugs me for what feels like forever. Just hugging for upwards of ten minutes while she cries and tells me she loves me. I uncomfortably accept this much-needed motherly affection while repeatedly grumbling that she's embarrassing me. She tells me she doesn't care and keeps holding on. She is really being such a total mom right now. We make our way from LAX back to my apartment, and the whole time she is going off like a bird. Squawking out question after question. "Where is your apartment?" "Are there supposed to be this many homeless people?" "What do you DO all day?" I give her the best lies I can muster because I don't want her to know the truth about my life. Thank goodness. She gets along great with Mar, and he is at the top of his game today. Complimenting my mother, telling her how wonderful I am. It truly is a lovely day. Except for the awful, terrible, no good, very bad guilt in my heart.

"Where is a good place to eat around here? I'm starving!" my mom says with a mischievous look on her face.

"Well, we have good Indian food," Mar helpfully pipes up, turning to look at her for a second before he turns back to the road.

"Let's go! I love Indian food!" She claps her hands together and smiles even bigger.

"Mom, I thought you hated Indian food." I carefully prod.

"That was your father. He hated everything. He would only eat Mexican food." She laughs heartily and pats my shoulder from the backseat.

"Let's not talk about dad." I lean on the dashboard and bury my head.

"Fine. Let's not talk about your dead, piece-of-shit father." With a huff, she sits back and crosses her arms.

I am shocked at her outburst as it's so not her. But she seems amped about being here so the adrenaline is making her goofy. "Mom!"

"What? Should we just forget about him? Because I would love to be able to." The smile returns to her face and she laughs at her own quip.

We pull up to the restaurant, and my mom practically dances out of the car, oohing and aahing at the neon-lit, hole-in-the-wall eatery. We go inside and order our curried foods and then find a table. I eat the naan like it's the end of the world, and Mar teases me for it. Mar excuses himself to the bathroom, and my mother gives me a loving look.

"He's better than Dylan and you-know-who." She side-eyes me as she takes another bite of food.

I bury my head in my hands, trying to be as small as possible. "I know. He's very sweet. He just wants me to say I love you. I don't know if I feel that way." I peek at her between my fingers and frown.

"You get loved the way you love yourself, Mushy. Just love yourself and it'll come to you." She pats me on the back and smiles.

"I just don't know if I can love myself after what I've done…" My mom looks quizzically at me and tilts her head. "Mom, I—" I choke on my words as I feel a presence behind me.

"Hey there, Kitty-cat." I turn and look around. It's John. He's pushing his beer gut into my face and looking down at me with a terrifyingly pleased smile. "I've been waiting to run into you."

I am terrified. Beyond terrified. One of the last interactions we had was him threatening our lives. "Please, John. No, I—" I lean back, and tears well up in my eyes.

"You owe me, and now I found you, you dumb fucking slut," he says, spitting in my face.

"This is not the time. In fact, never is the time," I say through gritted teeth. The tears start pouring down my face as hard as I try to sound and act tough.

He puts his hand on my shoulder and tightens his grip. "You fat little slut, I'm gonna leave you bleeding in a gutter." I yank myself from his grasp and prepare to defend myself. I don't know how far he is willing to go here in public.

"What the fuck did you say to my girlfriend?" Mar appears suddenly, leaving me feeling so relieved, and shoves John towards the door.

"You must be her friend. I'll fuck you up too." He goes to shove Mar back.

Mar swings and decks John right across the cheek. A weak blow, but one big enough to leave John speechless.

I turn to her and grab my mother's hand. "We gotta go, Mom," I hiss quietly.

"What about our food?" she squeaks innocently while looking around back and forth between us and John. "I don't understand what's happening, Mushy." She looks at me with confused eyes.

The waitress hands us our bagged food and points to the door. "Get the fuck out of my restaurant." That answers my mother's question and leaves us speechless.

We get up and hastily leave, grabbing a screaming Mar on the way. Mar was laying into John so hard it looked like John might start crying. The little bitch. We get in the car, and Mar squeals away from the curb. We race down 4th Street, and Mar lets out an angry throat gurgle. I turn to my mom, and she looks at me so startled, I just want to hug her.

"Why— What— Mushy…" Her face is darkened, and she's not nearly in as good of a mood as she was earlier.

"I've been selling my underwear on craigslist. That's a guy that harassed me so bad I stopped," I blurt out as fast as I can in fear that I'll never tell the truth about anything. There is a deafening silence in the car. I could cut the tension with a knife.

My mom breaks the silence. "Oh, Mushy. If you needed money you could've told me." Her face softens, and she reaches forward to rub my back.

"I didn't want to burden you," I quietly whisper, almost to myself.

My mom pushes my hair behind my ear and smiles sadly. "You are my everything, Michelle. I just want you to have a good life."

I smirk at her and roll my eyes like this is another embarrassing moment. "Okay, Mom, thank you for saying that. I appreciate you."

We pull up in front of my apartment, and my mom wraps her arms around my shoulders as we walk inside. She kisses me on the forehead and then grabs her food, sitting on the couch and patting the spot next to her. I sit down and so does Mar. We start eating in silence and I smile to myself. I have never felt so loved.

The rest of my mom's visit goes smoothly, she enjoys the sights and all the fun things Mar and I show her around Long Beach. We go to the beach, we go bowling, we do every touristy thing you can think of and more. Halfway through my mom's stay, I am summoned to interview at the Queen Mary, an old historic boat/hotel, and the interview seems to go well. I walk in with an air of as much confidence as I can muster since I know that it makes me much more appealing. The hiring manager laughs at a few of my jokes, and I am thrilled. They have to hire me, I am just so charming.

My mom is proud of me after hearing me regale her with the tale of my day and buys me a cactus as a celebration present. I love that stupid cactus. I'm terrified that I can't even water a cactus correctly, but I love it nonetheless. The whole trip though, I just want to get that one last thing off my chest. Just tell my mom and take the wrath that is to come. Even if it means she will think I am an awful brat, she deserves the truth. I can never find the right moment though. She is always so happy. I can't ruin that.

We are packing the day of her flight. It's four-thirty in the morning, and Mar is making us coffee. I grab my mom's hand as she folds her last shirt.

"Move out here, Mom." I put on my best doe eyes.

"Maybe one day, but not now. I still have my own mother and father to take care of." I sigh a sigh of sadness since I know she's right, but I want her to move here anyway.

We pack up the car and fill our mugs with hot, steaming coffee. We drive to the airport in mostly stillness while listening to some sad songs about sad shit that I put on because my mood is lower than ever. We pull up to the front of the terminal, and it's now or never.

"Mar, baby, can you please get out of the car?"

"Sure, babe."

Mar exits the car and starts unloading my mom's luggage from the trunk. My mom adjusts how she's sitting so that she is facing me. She grabs my hand, as she always does, and holds it tight. I start crying immediately. Through the sobs, I start to make out words.

"Mom…You know all these years I had all this money for no reason. Well, there was a reason. Dad was the reason." I cover my face with my hands and fill my palms with tears.

"I know, honey. Do you think I'm really so blind?" I see between my fingers that she looks at me with too kind of a face for what I just told her.

"But the reason he gave me the money was to keep quiet about his affairs." I am talking way too fast and I can feel every word barely forced out of my throat.

My mother gets very quiet and squeezes my hand even harder. She starts to sob too. "I know."

"You know?!" I lean back slightly and my jaw hangs open a bit. "Why didn't you ever get mad at me? Why don't you hate me?"

"How could I be mad at a confused teenager? I never brought it up because I love you. I love you no matter what. I'm just so happy that you trust that love so much that you would finally tell me."

I start crying even harder and lean my head against her shoulder. "I love you too, Mom. I'm so sorry," I choke out.

We hug and cry and cry and hug while a security guard angrily yells at Mar for being at the curb too long. The guard knocks on the window and makes motions with his hands as if to tell us to move or his forehead vein will explode.

My mom whispers her last words to me and she hugs me tight before exiting the car. "I love you more than life itself. I'll never stop, Michelle."

She shuts the door and grabs her luggage, flipping off the security guard while his back is turned, then entering the airport. I get out of the backseat and sit in the front while Mar gets back in on the driver's side. I lean against the window and watch my mom slowly disappear through the automatic doors as we drive away. I wipe the tears from my eyes.

"I love you, Mar."

About the Author

Alysa has been writing since 2000 when they started their first serial killer book and tantalized their classmates. This began a couple decades of writing screenplays, stage plays, comics, and books while attending art schools and later dropping out. Instead of continuing with academics, they embraced their love for everything creative—expanding their mind and fulfilling their spirit by creating constantly. These days, Alysa spends most of their time writing, doing freelance social media consulting work, and spending time with their dogs and husband. Don't think that they are living a quiet life though; they thrive on chaos.

They have been mentally ill since '91 when they were spit out into this tortuous world. Writing so their brain doesn't explode. A manic jumbled person with manic jumbled thoughts. Continuously trying to make life a little less lonely, one book at a time.

A lover of dogs, milkshakes, and the PNW. A dedicated karaoke artist. Maker of all things cute and cuddly. A nostalgia whore. Obsessed with the color orange and the '70s. Living proof that aliens exist. A comedian and a national treasure. Enigma of the highest order. Gummy candy is the best candy.